Finding a Way Through When Someone Close has Died

What it feels like and what you can do to help yourself

A workbook by young people, for young people

Pat Mood and Lesley Whittaker

Jessica Kingsley Publishers
London and Philadelphia

First published in the United Kingdom in 2001
by Jessica Kingsley Publishers
116 Pentonville Road
London N1 9JB, UK
and
400 Market Street, Suite 400
Philadelphia, PA 19106, USA

www.jkp.com

This book has been written by:

Ann	Stephanie
Kimberley	Charlotte
Russell	Kate
Claire	Zahra
Simon	Cassandra
Carly	Anna
Ryan	Matthew

With help and encouragement from:

Margaret   Barbara

Patricia   Pat   Lesley

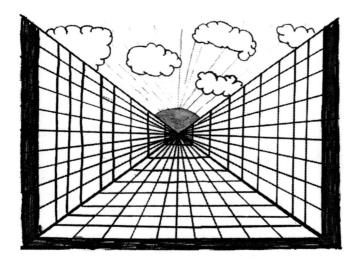

This book is dedicated to the courage of children and young people who are finding their way through when someone close has died

Dear Reader

When someone close to you dies you can feel very alone. Mixed-up feelings and thoughts may take you by surprise.

Everyone around is upset too, so it may seem as if there is no-one safe to turn to.

People may not know or understand how you feel. They may expect you to be grown-up, to talk when you don't want to, or not to show your feelings. Some people say hurtful things, sometimes intentionally.

You may have extra worries since your special person died, such as having less money, not being able to concentrate at school or feeling responsible for your parent or for someone else in the family.

All the young people who were involved in writing this workbook have gone through the experience of a parent or someone else close to them dying.

They want you to know that you are not alone, and they would like their words and drawings to help you.

They took part in a group which met to talk about how they were getting on, to ask questions, to deal with painful feelings and memories, and to have fun.

How you can use this workbook

The first part of the workbook is about **feelings and thoughts**. When the young people met each other they were surprised and then comforted to find that others felt the same as they did.

The next part of the book has **ideas for things you may find helpful** in finding your way through. Each of these has been of help to someone else after someone close has died.

At the end of the book you will find addresses of organizations you can contact for more help in finding your way through.

We hope that in reading this book you will learn that feelings are normal. Use the pages to draw or write about your own feelings and experiences. It can make them less painful. You can talk with someone you trust about what you have written or you can choose to keep it as a book that is private to you.

Lesley and Pat

Feelings,

Thoughts

and the

Way Things Change

After Someone Close Has Died...

When someone close has died your brain may feel overloaded by all the feelings

Ouch! Does your head feel like this sometimes?

What does your brain feel like?

Why not ease the pressure in your head by writing or drawing about it here?

Feelings just happen

You can't ignore them...

They can be all mixed up!

Here are some feelings
many people have...

Angry...

"Life is so unfair!"

"Everyone else still has the person they are close to, but **I don't!**"

"Sometimes I want to hit out and hurt some-one else, because they annoy me or for no particular reason."

Hearing friends talking about their family when someone in yours has died can make you very angry, especially when they seem not to love or appreciate them as much as you did.

You may feel resentful of others in the family for having fun when you are sad.

When someone dies it may seem as if they did not want to be with you, and you can feel angry with them for leaving you.

What makes me angry...

20

Frightened...

Being aware that life is so different can fill you with panic.

When someone close to you has died you may feel afraid it will happen to someone else, or even to all your family, leaving you on your own.

Feeling you have to watch over people in the family can be a worry. You may be afraid when adults in the family seem to be less capable, or not their usual selves, as if they might not get through it. You may feel responsible for keeping them going.

Lots of people are frightened for a while by bad memories, being alone in the dark, or by bad dreams and thoughts.
    They find it helps to write or draw about it, or to tell someone they trust. Then the fear seems to grow less and less.

Writing or drawing about your fears
can make them less powerful...

My fears...

Guilty...

Remembering the times when you thought or said something unkind, or when you did not do things to help, can make you feel guilty.

NOTHING ANYONE THINKS OR SAYS CAN MAKE SOMEONE DIE

but we often wish we had done more to tell or show someone that we loved them.

Guilty about having fun...

There are times when you are absorbed in doing something interesting or enjoyable and you may forget for a moment that someone special has died. Then you remember and feel bad for having forgotten and bad for having fun when something so sad has happened.

Lost and alone...

Not having that special person to talk to.

...others try to help but they don't know how it is for you, and that can make you feel alone.

You may keep your feelings from those who are close to you because you don't want to upset them more...

...so you feel even more alone.

Even though you know it cannot happen, you just want the person who has died to come back.

Embarrassed...

...about talking to people

...when people ask how you feel

...because you may feel you are different now

Add any other feelings
you have here

Feelings change over time...
...they come and go

from sunny and
cheerful.

to cold and miserable...

and many more in between.

Sometimes there are many different feelings
mixed up together...

And feelings change unexpectedly for no reason, or because of other things that happen.

at school

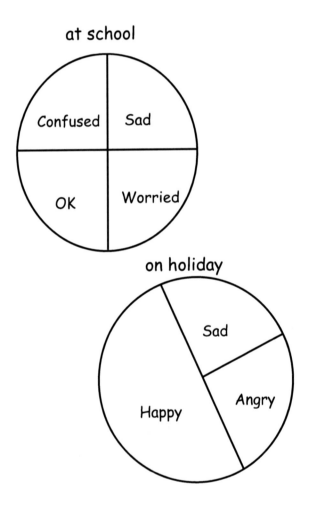

on holiday

You could put your feelings into a poem. This is what one of our group wrote:

Alone

I feel so alone since my mum died
I feel alone when nobody's there
It's not fair
My mum must have felt alone
When her dad died
It's not fair
I don't care
I'm alone because I'm an only child
It's not fair
I think of my mum when I cry
Why does it have to happen?
It's not fair.

by Ann

What are the thoughts and questions?

I thought he would always be there.

WHERE HAS SHE GONE?

IT'S NOT FAIR!

Is it my fault?

I wish I had not done or said what I did.

Why did this happen to me?

WHY DO PEOPLE SAY AWFUL THINGS?

I wanted him to see my children.

These were some of the thoughts we had.

More thoughts...

What will I say?

Facing everyone makes it more real.

What will other people say and think?

Because what has happened has made me feel different from everyone else, I worry that people may pick on me.

WHY?

Why do people die?

Couldn't we have kept him?

WHERE ARE THEY?

"Heaven is hard to imagine. I'm not sure of how to think of him as being now. People say he's looking down on me. I'm not sure whether he can hear and see everything I do – but somehow I know he is there."

I JUST WANT HIM/HER BACK!

Zahra wrote about her thoughts:

Death

I Think When You Die You Go To This Wonderful Place Where You Are Happy Not Sad. My Nana And Grandad And Uncle Must Be Happy There Where God Is Looking After Them And They Do Not Have Pain Any More.

I Think Heaven Is Red Because Red To Me Is A Happy Colour And When You Die You Are So Happy With God. I Feel There Is No Reason Why You Should Feel Afraid About Crying.

If There Was A Way To Get My Family That Have Died Back I Would Try And Get Them Back But There Isn't A Way To Get Them Back But I Wish There Was A Way To Get Them Back.

Why not write down some of your thoughts?

I wish...

"I wish I had showed her I loved her. I know that she knew that I did. When she was very ill I didn't hug her. Looking back I wish that I had."

Why not write about some of your wishes?

I wish...

I wish...

I wish...

Finding a way through
the difficult things

Everything has changed – what we talk about,
what we do, what we think about.

It often seems that the only way to cope is to
hide your feelings – like putting on a mask.

What difficult things do you have to cope with?

- Mealtimes may be different – not sitting down together, eating more junk food.
- Having less money.
- Having to go everywhere by bus.
- Having only one person to look after you.
- Not having time with that person, not having their help with homework, or just missing the fun you had together.

More difficult things...

- Not having the person you love around.
- Knowing that he or she will never be there again. You have to accept it, though you don't want to. Sometimes you can't believe it.
- Watching a parent get upset. Wondering what will happen.
- It seems as if the whole world has changed around you and nothing appears safe or dependable any more.

What are your most difficult things?

Making a list can make them less worrying.

What is the face on your mask?

- a brave smile?... a blank expression?... an angry glare?

Why not draw your real face,
the one the mask is hiding?

What about other people?

Other people can hurt you by what they say or do. Some don't realize they are hurting, some make spiteful remarks deliberately.

Family members may feel or show sadness differently, or at different times. Brothers, sisters or parents may not feel like sharing feelings, or they may want to talk when you don't.

It is easy for people in families to misunderstand or to get angry with each other.

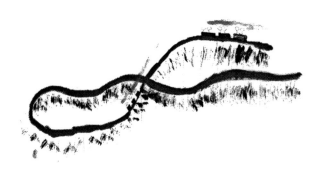

At school

"Sometimes teachers don't seem to see how hard it is for you to concentrate on work."

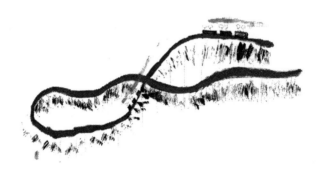

Outside home

"Some people don't care... Relatives disappear... Friends may be embarrassed and may avoid you. Some are helpful early on, but as time goes by they expect you to be back to normal."

Some unexpected people turn out to be understanding and may become new friends.

It all feels like being on a roller-coaster.

What are the ups and downs on your roller-coaster?

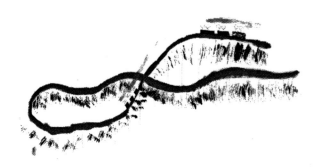

Where are you now?

How bad can it get?

- You may worry that someone else close to you, or that you will die.
- You may feel it is somehow your fault.
- You may find it difficult to leave the nightmares behind.
- There may be times when you cannot see an end to feeling lonely and unhappy. It may be easier not to go on, and you may be tempted to harm yourself.

What are the things that worry you?

Making a list can be the beginning of discovering ways of managing your worries.

My worst dream

Imagine a happy ending to your dream.

Draw or write it here so the dream becomes less scary.

What helps?

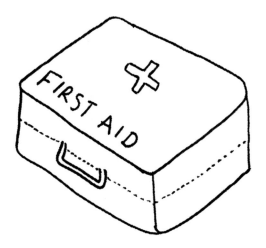

There are many things you can do to help yourself feel better. Why not make your own First Aid Box from some of the suggestions that follow? Each of them has helped someone else.

Remember that it is OK to feel sad and to cry

Crying lets some of the pain and sadness out.

Crying on your own can help, but sometimes crying with family members and friends can share the pain and help you feel you are not on your own.

Talking to friends

Although they might not fully understand some friends really want to help.

It is good to know that others care about you.

Writing or drawing

Keeping a diary or writing about something that has happened can be a good way of getting your feelings and thoughts out of your head.

You could invent a code, or make your writing messy so others can't read it. Maybe you won't need to read it again.

Remembering

Don't be afraid of memories. They are precious.

Death ends a person's bodily life but it doesn't end how special they are to you.

Read on to find ways of remembering...

Ways of remembering...

Photographs

It can be painful to see reminders of happier times or of someone who is no longer with you but photographs can help you to remember their love and all the happiness of the occasion.

They take you back to how it was then, how the person looked and sounded. You need especially to remember those things when there has been a long or difficult illness.

Things to treasure

Keeping special things can make you feel closer to the person who has died. These can be:

- Something they have given you

- Something that was theirs

- Something they have left specially for you

- Something that reminds you of a happy time you shared together

- Something that reminds you of them

Television, Videos, Games

Computer games, especially those about fighting and wrestling, can be a safe way of hitting out at imaginary people. It's like fighting against evil or the force that took them away.

Getting your anger out and letting off steam

Try finding safe ways to let off steam and get your feelings out.

- Punching a pillow
- Having a good run or a swim
- Writing a letter to the person who has died
- Playing music
- Having a good shout in a large open space
- Dancing

DON'T be tempted to do anything dangerous to you or anyone else.

Controlling dreams and nightmares

- The more you worry about them the more they seem to come.
- Talking about them can take the fear away.
- Finding another ending (a funny or happy one) can help.
- Remind yourself that they are only dreams and they cannot hurt you.
- Don't expect them to disappear immediately.

Joining a group

There are special groups to help young people when someone has died.

You can find out if there are any in your area by asking your doctor or by contacting the Children's Bereavement Project. The address and phone number is at the end of this workbook.

Turn to the next page to find out how groups help.

How groups help

You learn that there are others in the same situation as you and who feel the same as you do.

The activities help you to express your feelings and to find ways of remembering.

You can say what you really feel and think, and it's OK.

You learn how to deal with your feelings in a safe way and not to take it out on yourself.

You can ask about anything you don't understand.

You make new friends.

Talking to someone who really understands and asking about anything that bothers you

Talking to someone you can trust can help. It might be someone who is outside your situation so you can say exactly how you feel.

This could be someone whose job it is to help when someone has died, like a counsellor or a social worker.

Some questions do not have simple answers but in talking with someone else you may find your own answer.

If you are worried about yourself or someone else

You can speak to

- Your family doctor
- Your teacher
- A counsellor
- A social worker
- Someone from the list of people and organizations at the end of the workbook

Taking time out from grieving

Grieving is being very sad after someone has died.

It is quite OK and normal to think of other things and do other things that help to take your mind away from being sad all the time.

It's good to have fun.

Enjoying yourself doesn't mean that you don't care.

Taking time off from grieving helps you feel 'normal' again.

Looking after yourself

Try to eat well and get plenty of exercise.

Taking part in sport can bring new friends, get rid of tension and make you feel better.

Try not to cut yourself off from your family

Even though you sometimes lash out at them, and they at you, they are still always there.

It is important to spend time:
- Being together
- Finding ways to talk with them and sharing memories
- Being together for holidays, special days, meals, birthdays, days that are painful.

Remember – people in a family rarely feel and show their sadness in the same way.

The person who died was special to each of them, but maybe in different ways.

WHO IS ON YOUR FAMILY TREE?

Don't forget to include people who have died who are still important to you.

Do you know how others are feeling?

Do they know how you are feeling?

A letter from a teenager

"When everyone is upset after someone in the family has died, it's easy for children to be overlooked. The pain and sadness of losing someone like a parent can leave you not certain whether or not you want to talk. Part of grieving is private.

School:

can feel OK because it's a distraction from the sadness at home. Some school friends can be a help. If they are close friends they can be good at knowing when it is better to say something and when not to. But be prepared for some people at school saying things deliberately to upset you. Concentration is difficult sometimes and you find that your mind wanders. Keeping up with coursework and homework can be hard.

Sometimes it can feel so bad that it seems easier not to go on. You can end up by harming yourself and that isn't good."

FIND SOMEONE SAFE TO TELL, AND GET YOURSELF SOME SUPPORT.

As time goes on:

"The first anniversary can be difficult because you find yourself reliving the events and feelings of last year. It's not always clear that others in the family feel the same so it can seem that you are on your own with your sadness. It does get better when the immediate pain wears off. New hobbies and interests can help you to feel that life can be good.

What helps?

Being out, getting exercise, having fun, new friends."

KEEP GOING, DON'T QUIT!

Anna thought that everyone should know what it is like when someone close to you has died so she wrote this letter to the local paper.

"Some people may know how hard it is to lose someone they love very much but I'm still going to tell you about it as I think it's important to write about these things.

A person in your family may have died recently and it doesn't matter if they were old or young it is still upsetting.

You stay awake all night just crying over the person you loved.

If they were old and ill you knew it had to come soon but Why? you keep asking yourself, why did it happen this soon?

If the person who died was young it's very sad because he or she still had a life ahead of him or her. I bet you think why did it happen so soon?

It is sometimes a shock to hear the news. You had fun together but that fun will never end because that person lives in you still. And never forget that."

What would you say in a letter to the paper about what help a young person needs after someone close has died? When adults get things wrong or appear not to understand they might be glad of a few clues to help them learn how to help.

Who is there for me now?

People I can trust in my family, friends, teachers and others.

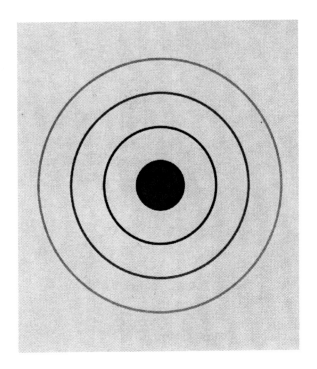

Put their names on or around the circles with those you trust most close to you.

My support system

I can laugh with . . . .

I can cry with . . . .

I can talk to . . . .

. . . . . . never lets me down

I can be my real self with . . .

. . . . cares about me

As time goes on...

You begin to see things in a different way.

You will probably find that you have become stronger, more understanding and better able to help others who lose someone close.

You learn that material things don't matter as much as they did.

You learn to see other points of view.

You begin to value the really important things in life.

You find you can look back with more happiness and less pain.

What are the important things you have learned?

A special memory

Make a drawing or use a photograph of your special person to help you to remember them and a happy time you had together.

Some memories may not be good but we learn that good and bad times are part of most people's lives.

There will be good times and difficult times in your life. Don't forget that the sun is still shining even when you can't see it!

Useful Information

Books to read

St Christopher's Hospice Bookshop stock most of the books listed. Telephone: 020 8778 9252.

For younger children

Someone Special has Died
St Christopher's Hospice

Granpa
John Burningham, Puffin

Remembering Mum
Ginny Perkins and Leon Morris, Black

Waterbugs and Dragonflies
Doris Stickney, Mowbrays

Badger's Parting Gifts
Susan Varley, Collins

Beginnings and Endings with Lifetimes
  in Between
Mellonie and Ingpen, Lion

John's Book
Jill Fuller, Lutterworth

Aarvy Aardvark Finds Hope
Donna O'Toole, Mountain Rainbow Publications

Bridge to Terabithia
Katherine Paterson, Puffin

Midge, Gill and Steve
J. Dainty, Church House Publishing

Has Someone You Know Died?
(a pocket book for children) Bereavement
   Care (available from: Linda Machin Rooms,
   The Dudson Centre, Hanley,
   Stoke-on-Trent ST1 5DD Telephone 01782
   683155)

For Older Readers

Your Parent has Died
St Christopher's Hospice

Straight Talk about Death
   for Teenagers
E. Grollman, Beacon Press

The Soul Bird
M Snunit, Robinson Press

Has Someone You Know Died?
(pocket book for teenagers) Bereavement
   Care (address above).

When Parents Die
Rebecca Abrams, Letts

Facing Grief – Bereavement
  and the Young Adult
Susan Wallbank, Lutterworth Press

For Reading With an Adult

Talking with Children and Young People
  about Death and Dying
Mary Turner, Jessica Kingsley Publishers

Talking About Death
Earl Grollman, Beacon Press

Board Games

All About Me
Peta Hemmings, Barnados Publications

The Grief Game
Jessica Kingsley Publishers

Organizations you can contact
To find out about groups and people who you can talk
to in the area where you live:

Childline 0800 1111
Childline is a free national helpline for children and
young people in danger and distress. It provides a
confidential phone counselling service for any child
with any problem 24 hours a day every day. Childline
listens, comforts and protects.

Minicom line for children and young people with hearing problems 0800 400 222 (Monday to Friday 9.30am to 9.30pm, Saturday and Sunday 9.30 am to 8pm)

The Line - a special helpline for children living away from home 0800 88 4444 (Monday to Friday 3.30pm to 9.30pm, Saturday and Sunday 2pm to 8pm)

Website - www.childline.org.uk

Childhood Bereavement Project
0115 911 8070

The project has a list of individuals and organizations providing individual and group support for bereaved children and young people in the UK.

The St Christopher's Candle Project

Telephone advice and consultancy to parents and professionals nationally, and individual and group counselling to children and families in the South London area.

The project has particular skills in working with sudden death.

Telephone 0208 778 9252 and ask for the Candle Project.

Bereavement Care: The Children and Families Project

The Children and Families Project is part of an independent charity that provides free support and counselling for bereaved children, young people and families in North Staffordshire; working individually, with families or in groups. Nationally they offer professional support, consultancy and training. **Telephone 01782 683155**

Winston's Wish

Provides a grief support programme for children and families living in Gloucestershire following a close family death. Camp Winston offers the opportunity to meet with others who have had a similar experience. Individual work is offered when grief is complicated.

Nationally, information, advice, publications and resources including a Charter for Bereaved Children are available by phone.

Winston's Wish Family Line 0845 20 30 40 5

Guidance and information for families of bereaved children.

www.winstonswish.org.uk